Scholarships for Middle Class Students

Strategies to Help Students Afford College and Reduce Student Loans

Also by Marianne Ragins

Winning Scholarships for College
College Survival & Success Skills 101

Scholarships *for* Middle Class Students

*Strategies to Help Students
Afford College and Reduce Student
Loans*

Marianne Ragins

TSW Publishing
P. O. Box 176
Centreville, Virginia 20122
www.scholarshipworkshop.com
TSW Publishing is a division of The Scholarship Workshop LLC

Copyright © 2020 by Marianne Ragins
All rights reserved. No part of this book may be used or reproduced in any manner whatsoever without prior written consent of the author, except as provided by the United States of America copyright law.

Scholarships for Middle Class Students was written to provide accurate advice to readers. However, please note that the author nor the publisher are engaged in the practice of providing legal, accounting, tax or other professional advice unless otherwise indicated. If you need legal, accounting, tax or other advice, please consult a professional in the appropriate area. Neither the author, the publisher, nor any entity associated with *Scholarships for Middle Class Students* assume any liability for errors, omissions, or inaccuracies. Any action you take or do not take as a result of reading *Scholarships for Middle Class Students* is entirely your responsibility.

ISBN: 978-1-950653-50-8

Printed in the United States of America

This book is available at special quantity discounts for bulk purchases for sales promotions, premiums, fundraising, and educational use. Special versions or book excerpts can also be created to fit specific needs.

For more information, please contact info@scholarshipworkshop.com or call 703 579-4245. You can also write: TSW Publishing, P. O. Box 176, Centreville, Virginia 20122.

Dedication

To my mother, my husband and my little ones;
your love, motivation, and presence in my life keep
me going.

For G. L. Solomon
As one who truly got the most from life
and helped us to get the most from ours,
your sunny smile, loving heart and
generous ways will be remembered forever
by all of your family and friends.

Contents

Introduction	11
Finding Specific Scholarships You Can Win	12
Exploring Scholarships, Awards and Prizes for Middle Class Students in Grades K - 12	22
Elementary School	25
Middle School Only	31
Middle and High School	33
Exploring Opportunities for Middle Class Students Currently in College	55
Searching for Additional Scholarships	64
Library Search	64
Internet Search	65
Local Search	69
Applications	72
Winning Elements	74
Essays	74
Your Work Samples	75
Articles	76
Résumé/Activity List	76
Recommendations	79
Crafting Your Essay	81
Other Strategies for Middle Class Students	88

Introduction

As an author who writes about getting college money, a successful scholarship winner, and as a workshop leader, I frequently get asked if there are scholarships for middle-class students. My answer is, yes, of course. Although there are many need-based scholarship programs, there are also numerous merit-based scholarship programs, awards, and contests.

Are you wondering how to find them? First, when reading through any of the lists of scholarships in books, scholarship directories, or program websites, the additional eligibility guidelines will usually state whether a program is need-based. Even if the guidelines do not indicate a program is need-based, applications requesting certain information such as annual income, a statement of financial need, or defining specific income levels based on family size, are probably for need-based aid. It is important to note that even though some programs may state that financial need is required, the definition of need can vary. So be very clear what determines financial need by thoroughly reviewing the program's site and the application. Ask additional questions if necessary. You should also be aware that some smaller community-based programs faced with few or no applicants and a strong desire to award an annual scholarship, may still award a deserving student without financial need, but who shows strong potential in terms of leadership and community service. In addition, some need-based programs may ask for a statement from you indicating why you should still be considered for a scholarship when you do not meet stated income limits. If given this opportunity, take it. Explain that care for extended family members, for example, or even residing in a high cost of-living area can really stretch an income.

Overall, the successful, organized student should apply for all scholarships for which he/she is eligible. Look for merit scholarships, awards, contests, and competitions that generally do not require a financial need statement. Be aware that when you read the fine print, some do. If it does not require too much additional time and it's a regional or community-based award, apply anyway. You may be the exception. Otherwise there are still plenty of merit-based opportunities for you as a middle-class student. You just need to do the research to find them.

Finding Specific Scholarships You Can Win

You should make an effort to find scholarships specific to you and your family. Although some of the opportunities you find may have a need-based component, others do not. You can start exploring specific scholarships by asking yourself the following questions:

What are your hobbies?

Introduction

There are many scholarships for people who have particular hobbies. Books with extensive scholarship listings will have special sections dealing with these types of scholarships. Look for these special sections during your scholarship search. Some scholarship directories will title this section as extracurricular activities. An example of a scholarship or award that focuses on your hobbies would be the Pokémon World Championships (https://www.pokemon.com/us/play-pokemon —see *World Championships*). Players can win up to $25,000 in scholarships or cash.

If you are currently employed, where do you work? Contact the personnel or human resources office of your employer to inquire about scholarship opportunities and tuition reimbursement programs. If your company does not have a personnel office, speak with the general manager about the possibility of scholarship opportunities, or contact the company's general headquarters to learn if such opportunities exist. Many companies offer tuition reimbursement programs as an employee benefit. In tuition reimbursement, the employee initially pays the cost of tuition and fees for the courses taken in college or graduate school. Once the courses are completed and a satisfactory grade has been earned by the employee, the company/employer will then reimburse all or part of the tuition and fees initially paid by the employee. Some companies pay these costs

Scholarships for Middle Class Students

upfront. As a student working at Wendy's Old-Fashioned Hamburgers in high school, I was eligible for a Wendy's scholarship which I applied for and won.

For what company or companies do your parents currently work?

Ask your parents to contact their company personnel or human resources department to inquire if there are scholarships available to the children of employees. If the company does not have a personnel office, your parent should speak with the general manager about the possibility of scholarship opportunities or contact the company's general headquarters. Scholarship directories also list companies that sponsor scholarship programs for the children of their employees. You can also check books or online directories such as *The Foundation Directory Online* (https://fconline.foundationcenter.org), to learn whether your parent's company has a foundation set up to disburse scholarship money to the children of their employees or for other purposes. For example, Johnson Controls, Inc., maintains the Johnson Controls Foundation that offers scholarships to its employees' children.

Do you belong to a religious organization; for example, a church or synagogue?

Many religious organizations give scholarships not only to members of their congregations but to nonmembers as well. Some of them stipulate that

Introduction

the recipients of their scholarships must attend a college or university established to operate under the edicts of their denominational faith, such as a Presbyterian college or university. An example of this type of scholarship would be the Presbyterian Scholarships (http://www.presbyterianmission.org) offered to students who are members of the Presbyterian Church and are planning to attend a college related to the Presbyterian Church (U.S.A). Contact churches and religious organizations to inquire about scholarships such as these. You can also look in scholarship directories for the sections based on religious affiliations. In addition, speak with the minister of the church that either you and/or your parents attend. Most churches are more than willing to establish a small scholarship fund for their students. For instance, the church I was a member of in Macon, Georgia, Stubbs Chapel Baptist Church, gave me a small scholarship to attend college and also gave me money every year while I was enrolled.

Are you a child or close relative of a war veteran? If so, in which war and in what branch of service did your relative serve?

Numerous scholarships are available for children and close relatives of veterans who served in specific wars, such as World War II. Books with extensive scholarship listings will have special sections dealing with these types of scholarships. The sections may be titled "Armed Forces" or

"Military." You will need to know the branch of the Armed Forces in which your relative served to find scholarships that apply specifically to you. Examples of these scholarships are those offered by the Military Benefit Association, which provides scholarships to its members who serve in the military (http://www.militarybenefit.org). The Fisher House Foundation's website (http://www.militaryscholar.org) is another resource for scholarship information associated with the military.

Are you a veteran or a disabled veteran?
Scholarship and financial assistance is available to most disabled veterans, especially from the government. If you are a disabled veteran, contact the Federal Student Aid Information Center (800-433-3243), visit StudentAid.gov to inquire about scholarship opportunities, or call the Department of Veterans Affairs (800-827-1000; http://www.va.gov or http://www.gibill.va.gov). You may find governmental organizations with programs that pay for tuition, fees, books, and equipment of veterans disabled during active duty and honorably discharged. To find financial aid such as this, look in the "Military Disabled" or "Armed Forces" sections of the scholarship guides.

Are you legally blind or do you have any other disabilities?
Students who are legally blind or in some other way disabled can usually receive scholarships and

Introduction

financial aid assistance from many sources, especially the government. During your search, look for directories that have special sections dealing with scholarships for the disabled. The American Council of the Blind (http://www.acb.org) currently offers scholarships to students who are legally blind.

Are you related to someone with a disability or who is a survivor of a disease?

For example, if your parent is deaf or hard-of-hearing, the Millie Brother Scholarship for Hearing Children of Deaf Adults is offered through Children of Deaf Adults (CODA) (www.coda-international.org). There are also scholarships for survivors of certain diseases such as cancer. Currently the Dr. Angela Grant Memorial Scholarship Fund awards scholarships to cancer survivors or those within the immediate family of a cancer survivor (http://www.drangelagrantscholarship.org). This is an area where an advanced Internet search, could be helpful to you in finding college aid specific to your situation, disease, or disability.

For minority groups other than African American, can you trace your lineage? (For example, Samoan, Japanese, Native American, etc.)

Many programs have scholarships strictly for minorities of a certain descent. To win these scholarships you may be required to prove your lineage. Look for scholarships such as these if you fall into this category. An example of this type of

Scholarships for Middle Class Students

scholarship would be the scholarships offered by the Welsh Society of Philadelphia to students of Welsh descent (http://www.philadelphiawelsh.org). To be eligible to receive this scholarship, applicants must prove their lineage and enroll in a college within 100 miles of Philadelphia.

Are you or your parents a member of a union, trade group, or association?

If you or your parents are members of a union, trade group, or association, you may be eligible to win scholarships such as the E. C. Hallbeck Memorial Scholarship offered by the American Postal Workers Union (http://www.apwu.org) to high school seniors who are dependents of active or deceased members of the union. Or consider the scholarship program from Union Plus (http://www.unionplus.org), an organization established by the AFL- CIO to provide consumer benefits to members and retirees of participating labor unions.

What are you strongly interested in studying at college?

Scholarships are available to students interested in a particular major. If you are certain of your intended major, look for directories and scholarship opportunities in that area. For students interested in the field of health care, for example, the Tylenol Future Care Scholarship program (https://www.tylenol.com/news/scholarship) is available, or consider reviewing scholarships offered by the American Medical Association Foundation (http://www.ama-assn.org). The scholarships don't

Introduction

just stop at health care or medicine—you can find other associations for scholarships in other fields. Use a scholarship directory or perform an advanced Internet search to find scholarships related to your current or future major.

Are you a member of a fraternity or sorority? Many sororities and fraternities sponsor scholarships. For instance, members of Theta Delta Chi can apply for scholarships, and the Alpha Kappa Alpha Sorority, Inc., Educational Advancement Foundation also offers several scholarships, including some that are open to nonmembers. As you look through scholarship directories, look for scholarships sponsored by a fraternity or sorority. If you are unable to discover any, write or call the national chapter of your organization, or visit its website, Facebook, or other social media platforms to uncover opportunities. In fact, local sororities and fraternities will often contact me (author of this book) to help them advertise a scholarship program that may be suffering from a low application rate.

Are your parents' members of a fraternity or sorority? Some sororities and fraternities sponsor scholarships for the children of their members. As you look through scholarship directories, look for scholarships sponsored by your parents' fraternity or sorority. If you are unable to discover any, write to the national chapters of the organizations or visit their website, Facebook, or other social media platforms, if available. You can also do an advanced Internet search.

Are your parents' alumni of a college or university? Many colleges and universities offer scholarships to the children of their alumni. Contact the college or university they attended to inquire about scholarship opportunities that may be available to you.

Where do you live? Have you checked for community foundations in your area? Numerous scholarships are offered by organizations and companies to students who live in a specific area, usually where the company or organization is located or does business. To find scholarships in this category, do an advanced Internet search to find community foundations, county websites, or school websites with scholarships specific to your area. Use search terms such as "scholarships" and the name of your county, city, or state to find scholarships in local areas. Also do the same for "scholarships" and the search words "community foundation" along with the name of your city, county, or state to uncover community foundations in your area. For example, the Community Foundation of Northern Virginia (https://www.cfnova.org), the Berks County Community Foundation in Pennsylvania (http://www.bccf.org), and the Community Foundation of Central Georgia (http://www.cfcga.org) are all examples of community-based foundations that serve a specific community or a group of communities within a specific region.

What are your extracurricular activities?
Activities such as participation in Distributive Education Club of America (DECA; http://www.deca.org), Future Business Leaders of America (FBLA; http://www.fbla-pbl.org), the National Honor Society (NHS; http://www.nhs.us), and Junior Achievement (http://www.ja.org) may allow you to become eligible for scholarships from these organizations or as members of these organizations. For example, high school seniors who are members of DECA are eligible for renewable Harry A. Applegate Scholarships, for use in pursuing business education.

1

Exploring Scholarships, Awards and Prizes for Middle Class Students in Grades K - 12

Imagine having a scholarship or an award won before you become a high school senior? This could mean extra freedom for you when you do reach the pinnacle, your final year of high school. Then you could devote all of your time to being a senior and focusing on your dream college or university. Of course, scholarships and awards change every year but currently there are scholarships and awards you can win as early as age 6, particularly if you have already started volunteering and helping out in the community.

Scholarships and money available for younger students is often associated with prize winnings for art, writing, speaking or other talent contests such as the *American Legion National High School Oratorical Contest* and the *Doodle 4 Google* contest. Or, the money is associated with outstanding community service such as the *Jesse Brown Memorial Youth Scholarship Program*. Too, there are scholarships associated with recognizing exceptional talent or scientific interests early, such as the *Davidson Fellows Scholarship*. Not only are

1 – Exploring Scholarships in Grades K - 12

these great opportunities for younger students as well as high school seniors, they also give middle class students with little financial need a chance to win them as well, since they are based on factors other than financial need.

If you're a parent reading this publication and you're grooming your son or daughter to have the best chances of getting scholarship or prize money to help with college early, encourage them to explore their creative and scientific side. Also help them to understand the importance of giving back. A focus on both will boost their opportunities for scholarships as a young student but also for scholarships as high school senior. In addition, it will help improve their applications for entrance into competitive colleges and universities.

Middle class students with little or no need will also benefit from participating in community service and exploration into potential special talents. Many of the scholarships and awards for younger students as mentioned earlier in this chapter have no financial need requirements.

If you win a scholarship before you actually start your college studies, the money is usually held for you by the sponsoring organization. Once you notify the organization with information about your college or university, funds are often dispersed directly to the school. There are some awards you can win that are not technically considered scholarships and the funds may be sent directly to you immediately after you win. This

Scholarships for Middle Class Students

information is normally included in the sponsor's program materials or website. If funds are remitted directly to you, save! Don't spend! Or, if necessary, the funds could be spent to help pay for a current year's private school tuition, if you believe the benefits of the money being used for private school now outweigh the benefits of helping to pay for college later.

To help give you a jumpstart on money you can win before your 12th grade year, the following section includes a list of opportunities you can start pursuing even before you leave kindergarten or branch out from middle school.

The following awards and scholarships are general. They can be used for most majors and career fields and a variety of students are eligible to apply for them. Please contact each organization to confirm or update deadlines and eligibility criteria. Under no circumstances should you use this listing as the sole resource for your scholarship search. The purpose of this publication is to help you find scholarships that are specific to your situation and to show you steps to help you win them. The provision of the following list of scholarships is meant only to give you a jump-start on the scholarship process.

All of the following awards and scholarships are achievement based. They can be won by middle class students without regard to financial need.

1 – Exploring Scholarships in Grades K - 12

> ### *A Few Important Items to Remember*
> - Do not rely solely on the following scholarship list. It is best to use the strategies described in the chapter, "Searching for Additional Scholarships" to uncover the most opportunities available to you.
> - Some programs change their application requirements and eligibility guidelines. Please review their websites carefully for any changes.
> - Programs can and do stop awarding scholarships or suspend their scholarship programs. Don't get discouraged. You can still find available scholarships. But please know that there are no guarantees about the availability of a given scholarship, or that you will win it.
> - Follow us on Facebook (http://www.facebook.com/scholarshipworkshop) and Twitter (@ScholarshipWork) for frequent alerts on new scholarships and upcoming deadlines. Join our mailing list to get the latest updates about scholarships and other helpful information. Text "SCHOLARSHIPINFO" to 22828 or visit our website to join.

Elementary School

Davidson Fellows Scholarship

Website: http://www.davidsongifted.org/fellows or http://www.davidsonfellows.org

Additional Information: The Davidson Fellows scholarships range from $10,000 to $50,000 for students age 18 and under who have completed a significant piece of work. The program looks for students whose projects are at, or close to, the college-graduate level with a depth of knowledge in their particular area of study. The application categories are Science, Technology, Engineering, Mathematics, Literature, Music, Philosophy, and Outside the Box. To apply you must be a U.S. citizen or a permanent resident residing in the

Scholarships for Middle Class Students

United States, or be stationed overseas due to active U.S. military duty. There is no minimum age for eligibility. See website for specific details and guidelines for entering this competition.

Doodle 4 Google

Website: www.google.com/doodle4google
Additional Information: Doodle 4 Google is an annual program that encourages K-12 students in the United States to use their artistic talents to think big and redesign the Google homepage logo for millions to see. Previous themes have been "My Best Day Ever…" and "What I Want to Do Someday…" Winning student artists will see their artwork appear on the Google homepage, receive a $30,000 college scholarship, and a $50,000 technology grant for their school along with other prizes. Visit the website for complete eligibility guidelines, templates, and submission information.

The Gloria Barron Prize for Young Heroes

Website: https://barronprize.org
Additional Information: Each year, the Gloria Barron Prize for Young Heroes honors outstanding youth leaders ages 8 to 18 who have made a significant positive difference to people and the environment. Top winners in this program receive a $10,000 cash award to support their service work or higher education. The deadline is usually in

1 – Exploring Scholarships in Grades K - 12

April. Visit the website for additional information about references, application requirements and other details.

Jesse Brown Memorial Youth Scholarship Program

Disabled American Veterans
Website: http://www.dav.org (search *Jesse Brown Youth Memorial Scholarship*) or link to
http://www.dav.org/volunteers/Scholarship.aspx
Additional Information: The Jesse Brown Memorial Youth Scholarship Program was established to recognize youth volunteers age 21 or younger who have volunteered for a minimum of 100 hours at a VA medical center during the previous calendar year. You must be nominated for this program and write a 750 word essay entitled "What Volunteering Has Meant to Me." You can also nominate yourself. See the website for additional eligibility criteria, current deadlines and the nomination form. Scholarship amounts can be up to $20,000.

Optimist International Oratorical Contest

Website: http://www.optimist.org (see *Home \ Members \ Scholarship Contests*)
Additional Information: This scholarship is based on your ability to prepare and present a four to five minute speech on a specific topic within a timed period. Contestants, who must be no more than 19

Scholarships for Middle Class Students

years of age at the time of contest entry, must speak about the official oratorical contest subject which changes each year. For example, one year's contest subject was, "Why My Voice is Important." Contest is open to citizens of the US, Canada and the Caribbean. You must enter the contest through your local Optimist Club. To get contact information for your local Optimist club, visit the website. Students must compete in several levels. Visit the website for more details. Award amounts range up to $2,500.

Author's Personal Note: I competed in the Optimist International Oratorical Contest for several years at various levels beginning in the sixth grade, usually winning at each level but not the final level. Although I did not win the $1,500 award available at that time, I did gain invaluable experience in public speaking and in writing speeches which also helped me to write essays. These are very important skills to have especially if you want to win scholarships. It will help you in both interviews (the ability to speak well in public) and in preparing essays.

Optimist International Essay Contest

Website: http://www.optimist.org (see *Home\Members\Scholarship Contests*)
Additional Information: This is a multi-level essay writing contest. Student winners at the district and international level win scholarships. Contestants

1 – Exploring Scholarships in Grades K - 12

must be no more than 19 years of age at the time of contest entry. Contest is open to citizens of the US, Canada and the Caribbean. You must enter the contest through your local Optimist Club. To get contact information for your local Optimist club, visit the website for more details.

Profile in Courage Essay Contest

Website: www.jfklibrary.org
Additional Information: In recognition of one of President Kennedy's most important legacies, this contest is designed to promote the involvement of young people in the civic life of their country. High school students in the 9th through 12th grades can participate in this essay contest, by writing a compelling 1000 word (maximum) essay and citing at least five sources on the meaning of political courage. Registration forms must be submitted with the essay and are available on the website. The first place winner and the nominating teacher will be invited to receive awards at the Kennedy Library in Boston. Awards range from $500 to $10,000. The contest deadline is usually in January of each year.

The Prudential Spirit of Community Awards

Website: http://spirit.prudential.com
Additional Information: This program, sponsored by Prudential in partnership with the National

Scholarships for Middle Class Students

Association of Secondary School Principals (NASSP), recognizes students in grades 5 – 12 who have demonstrated exemplary community service. Local honorees are selected at participating schools and organizations in November, and from these winners, two state honorees are chosen from each state and the District of Columbia. State honorees receive an award of $1,000, an engraved silver medallion, and an all-expenses-paid trip to Washington, D.C. National honorees receive an additional award of $5,000, an engraved gold medallion, a crystal trophy for their school or organization and a $5,000 grant from The Prudential Foundation for a non-profit, charitable organization of their choice. Although this program is not officially a scholarship, the funds you win, if you're an avid volunteer, could add nicely to the money in your college fund to pay for your educational expenses.

Scripps National Spelling Bee

Website: https://spellingbee.com
Additional Information: The Scripps National Spelling Bee contest is open to elementary and middle school students who participate in the spelling bee competition. Student champions can win up to $50,000.

Sodexo Foundation

Stephen J. Brady STOP Hunger Scholarships
Website:://us.stop-hunger.org/home.html or http://www.sodexofoundation.org (see *Grants and Scholarships*)
Additional Information: Stephen J. Brady STOP Hunger Scholarships are open to students in kindergarten through graduate school who are enrolled in an accredited educational institution in the United States. The scholarships are available to students who have performed unpaid volunteer services impacting hunger in a community within the United States at least within the last 12 months. Additional consideration is given to students working to fight childhood hunger. A Community Service Recommendation is required for this application form so ask recommenders (who must not be family members) for their recommendations early.

Middle School Only

Angela Award

National Science Teachers Association
Website: www.nsta.org (search for *Angela Award*)
Additional Information: Female students in grades 5–8, who are involved in or have a strong connection to science, can be nominated for this award. The award was established in honor of Gerry Wheeler, Executive Director Emeritus, to recognize his outstanding dedication to the

Scholarships for Middle Class Students

National Science Teachers Association and lifelong commitment to science education. The award is a $1,000 US EE Savings Bond or Canadian Savings Bond purchased for the equivalent issue price.

Mathcounts

Website: www.mathcounts.org
Additional Information: Mathcounts is a middle school series of programs that include a mathematics competition and a math video challenge contest. In the mathematics competition, students have a chance to win a $20,000 scholarship. In the video contest, students can win up to $1,000.

Patriot's Pen Competition

Veterans of Foreign Wars
Website: www.vfw.org (search for *Youth Scholarships*)
Additional Information: Students must write an essay expressing their views on a patriotic theme that changes annually. The contest is sponsored by the Veterans of Foreign Wars Organization (VFW). Awards range from $500 to $5,000. The contest is open to students in grades 6 through 8.

Middle and High School

American Legion National High School Oratorical Contest

Website: http://www.legion.org (see *Programs\Family and Youth\Oratorical Contest*)
Additional Information: Open to students in grades 9 through 12 who are less than 20 years of age (as of the national contest deadline) and are U.S. citizens or lawful permanent residents of the United States. You must be currently enrolled in a high school or middle school (public, parochial, military, private, or state-accredited homeschool) in which the curriculum is considered to be of high school level. You must be able to prepare and deliver speeches in public to win these awards. In addition to the scholarships awarded by the national headquarters, several hundred scholarships may be awarded by intermediate organizations to participants at the post, district, county, or department levels of competition. Visit the website for more details and current deadlines. Award amounts range from $1,500 to $18,000.

Ayn Rand's Novelette Anthem Essay Contest

Website: www.aynrand.org (see *Students/Essay Contests*)
Additional Information: Open to 8th, 9th and 10th grade high school students who submit an essay of 600 to 1200 words. Awards up to $2,000.

Scholarships for Middle Class Students

Ayn Rand's Novel The Fountainhead Essay Contest

Website: www.aynrand.org (see *Students/Essay Contests*)
Additional Information: Open to 11th and 12th grade high school students who submit an essay of 800 to 1600 words. Awards range from $50 to $10,000.

C-Span's Student Cam

Website: http://www.studentcam.org
Additional Information: StudentCam is an annual national video competition from C-SPAN that encourages students to think critically about issues that affect the nation and its communities. To enter this competition you must be in grades 6-12 and create a short (5-6 minute) video documentary on a topic related to the yearly competition theme. You can compete individually or in teams of either two or three members and your video documentary must include clips of supporting C-SPAN video relating to the topic. Up to $100,000 in cash prizes are awarded.

The Christophers Annual Poster Contest for High School Students

Website: https://www.christophers.org/poster-contest

1 – Exploring Scholarships in Grades K - 12

Additional Information: In this yearly contest, students enrolled in the 9th through 12th grades can submit a poster interpreting the theme, "You Can Make a Difference." Prizes range from $100 to $1,000.

Cameron Impact Scholarship

Website: https://www.bryancameroneducationfoundation.org/cameron-impact-scholarship

Additional Information: The Cameron Impact Scholarship is a four-year merit based scholarship available to high school seniors. It covers full tuition and 'qualified educational expenses' (as defined by the Internal Revenue Service) at the recipient's chosen collegiate institution (estimated to be between $20,000-$50,000 per year).

Coca-Cola Scholars Foundation

Website: https://www.coca-colascholars.org

Additional Information: Scholarships are achievement-based and selection of winners is based on consideration of the applicant's leadership, character, achievement, and commitment, both inside and outside the classroom. Scholarships can be used for any field of study. According to the organization, "The kind of students that become Coca-Cola Scholars are ones that belong to a diverse group of outstanding

Scholarships for Middle Class Students

young people, characterized by their ability, commitment, perseverance, and determination. They share a 'special something else,' giving back in unselfish ways, embodying service over self, and are already finding ways to make a difference in society. By supporting these students, Coca-Cola, too, is giving back to the communities that have supported it for more than 100 years." In 2018, the Coca-Cola Scholars Foundation welcomed its 30th class of Coke Scholars. With this class, the foundation has provided over 6,000 scholars with more than $66 million in educational support.

To apply for the Coca-Cola scholarship, you must be a current high school senior attending school (or homeschooled) in the United States, a U.S. citizen, permanent resident, refugee, asylee, Cuban-Haitian entrant, or humanitarian parolee (based on guidelines utilized by the U.S. Department of Education for Federal Financial Aid eligibility), planning to pursue a degree at an accredited U.S. post- secondary institution. The initial application is available online. Selection of recipients for these scholarships occurs in phases, beginning in late summer each year with an initial online application, proceeding to a semifinalist stage with an interview and culminating the following spring with the announcement of the award recipients. Scholarships awarded are $20,000. The deadline to apply online is usually October 31 of each year.

1 – Exploring Scholarships in Grades K - 12

Author's Personal Note: I won a Coca-Cola National Scholarship, and the competition was one of the best and most organized I entered. In chapter 11 of *Winning Scholarships for College*, I included the essay I submitted in my semifinalist materials. I also have letters from the organization when I became a semifinalist and a finalist in chapter 28.

College JumpStart Scholarship

Website: www.jumpstart-scholarship.net
Additional Information: This scholarship is open to 10th through 12th grade high school students, college students and non-traditional students who are U.S. citizens or legal residents. You must be attending or planning to attend an accredited 2-year, 4-year or vocational/trade school in the U.S. and be committed to using education to better your life and that of your family and/or community.

College Is Power Scholarship

Website:
http://www.collegeispower.com/scholarship.cfm
Additional Information: This scholarship is available to students 17 years of age or older who plan to start a program of higher education within the next twelve months or who are currently enrolled in a program of higher education. You must be a full- or part-time student, attend a campus-based or online program and be a citizen

or permanent resident of the United States. Award amount is $1,000.

Courage in Student Journalism Awards

Student Press Law Center
Website: http://www.kent.edu/csj/courage-student-journalism-awards or visit www.kent.edu and search for, *Courage in Student Journalism Awards*
Additional Information: Open to middle and high school students who have stood in support of the First Amendment. Students must be nominated but you can also nominate yourself. Awards are up to $1000. See website for additional details.

Courageous Persuaders

Website: http://courageouspersuaders.com
Additional Information: Students in grades 9 through 12 in teams or individually, can create commercials up to 30 seconds long about the dangers of underage drinking or the dangers of texting while driving. The commercials are intended for middle school audiences and will be judged on originality, creativity and persuasiveness. Winners can receive up to $2,000 and students can enter separate videos in both categories.

1 – Exploring Scholarships in Grades K - 12

Create-A-Greeting Card Scholarship Contest

Website: www.gallerycollection.com/greetingcardscontests.htm or www.gallerycollection.com/greeting-cards-scholarship.htm

Additional Information: This $10,000 scholarship contest is open to all high school AND college students AND members of the armed forces who are enrolled during the time-period of the contest in an academic program designed to conclude with the awarding of a diploma or a degree. To participate, applicants must create a design for a Christmas card, holiday card, birthday card or all-occasion greeting card. Legal residents of the fifty (50) United States, the District of Columbia, American Samoa, Guam, the Commonwealth of the Northern Mariana Islands, the U.S. Virgin Islands, and Puerto Rico are eligible to enter. International students who have a student visa to attend school in the United States are considered legal residents and are also eligible to enter.

Davidson Fellows Scholarship

Davidson Institute for Talent Development
Website: http://www.davidsongifted.org/fellows or http://www.davidsonfellows.org

Additional Information: The Davidson Fellows scholarships range from $10,000 to $50,000 for students age 18 and under who have completed a significant piece of work. The program looks for students whose projects are at, or close to, the college-graduate level with a depth of knowledge in their particular area of study. The application categories are Science, Technology, Engineering, Mathematics, Literature, Music, Philosophy, and Outside the Box. To apply you must be a U.S. citizen or a permanent resident residing in the United States, or be stationed overseas due to active U.S. military duty. There is no minimum age for eligibility. See website for specific details and guidelines for entering this competition.

Doodle 4 Google

Website: www.google.com/doodle4google
Additional Information: Doodle 4 Google is an annual program that encourages K-12 students in the United States to use their artistic talents to think big and redesign the Google homepage logo for millions to see. Previous themes have been "My Best Day Ever…" and "What I Want to Do Someday…" Winning student artists will see their artwork appear on the Google homepage, receive a $30,000 college scholarship, and a $50,000 technology grant for their school along with other prizes. Visit the website for complete eligibility guidelines, templates, and submission information.

1 – Exploring Scholarships in Grades K - 12

DoSomething.Org Easy Scholarship Campaigns

Website: http://www.dosomething.org (see *Scholarships* section on the website)

Additional Information: DoSomething.org is a nonprofit for young people focused on social change for causes such as bullying, homelessness, and cancer. To apply for a scholarship, you need to complete a campaign and prove it with pictures of you in action during the campaign. They have many campaigns featured on the website. The scholarship program is open to U.S. and Canadian citizens 25 and under and does not require a minimum GPA. Winners are chosen through a random drawing.

Executive Women International Scholarship Program (EWISP)

Website: http://www.ewiconnect.com (see *Scholarships*)

Additional Information: Available to high school seniors who live within the boundaries of a participating chapter. You must be nominated by your high school for this award, which currently ranges from $1,000 to $4,000. Competition starts at the chapter level. Visit the website for additional information, deadlines, and to locate a participating chapter.

Scholarships for Middle Class Students

The Gloria Barron Prize for Young Heroes

Website: www.barronprize.org
Additional Information: Each year, the Gloria Barron Prize for Young Heroes honors outstanding youth leaders ages 8 to 18 who have made a significant positive difference to people and our planet. Top winners in this program receive a $10,000 cash award to support their service work or higher education. You must be nominated for this prize. Visit the website for additional information about nominations, application requirements and other details.

HOTH SEO Scholarship Program

Website: https://www.thehoth.com/seo-scholarship
Additional Information: HOTH is offering current college students and high school seniors accepted to an accredited university an opportunity to win a $1,000 scholarship. To enter, students must write an essay with a minimum of 1000 words on the topic of, "How Companies Can Take Advantage of Digital Marketing." For more details, visit the website.

Jesse Brown Memorial Youth Scholarship Program

Disabled American Veterans
Website: http://www.dav.org (search *Jesse Brown Youth Memorial Scholarship*) or link to http://www.dav.org/volunteers/Scholarship.aspx

1 – Exploring Scholarships in Grades K - 12

Additional Information: The Jesse Brown Memorial Youth Scholarship Program was established to recognize youth volunteers age 21 or younger who have volunteered for a minimum of 100 hours at a DAV or DAV facility such as a VA medical center during the previous calendar year. You must be nominated for this program and write a 750-word essay titled "What Volunteering Has Meant to Me." You can also nominate yourself. See the website for additional eligibility criteria, current deadlines, and the nomination form. Scholarship amounts can be up to $20,000.

Law Offices of Randolph Rice Scholarship

Website: https://ricelawmd.com/about/scholarship/
Additional Information: The Law Offices of Randolph Rice Scholarship awards a $1,500 scholarship each year to rising sophomores, juniors, or seniors who are enrolled at a four-year institution of higher learning, or a high school senior who has committed to attend an accredited U.S. college or university. Applicants must use data from government, private agencies or non-profits, to create an infographic and submit it to enter this scholarship competition. Infographics will be judged based on originality, creativity, and proper use of sources.

Scholarships for Middle Class Students

"Leading the Future II" Scholarship

Website: http://www.scholarshipworkshop.com
Additional Information: The "Leading the Future" Scholarship is designed to elevate students' consciousness about their future and their role in helping others once they receive a college degree and become established in a community. It is open to high school seniors or current college undergraduates who are U.S. residents. Visit the website to apply online.

National Honor Society Scholarship

Website: http://www.nhs.us or https://www.nhs.us/advisers/the-nhs-scholarship
Additional Information: Open to high school seniors who are members in good standing of the National Honor Society (NHS). Contact your NHS advisor for information about obtaining applications. Scholarship amounts range from $3,200 to $25,000. *Note:* The website makes the following comment about financial need, "It is important to note that scholarship selection is based on the four pillars of NHS—scholarship, service, leadership, and character—and financial need is also a consideration. The indication of need is not exclusionary. If a student does not demonstrate financial need, he/she is still eligible to apply for, and possibly be awarded, a scholarship."

1 – Exploring Scholarships in Grades K - 12

National Merit Scholarship Program

Website: http://www.nationalmerit.org
Additional Information: Applicants must qualify for this competition by taking the PSAT/NMSQT in the specified year of the high school program and no later than the third year in grades 9 through 12, regardless of grade classification or educational pattern. This usually means you should take the test in your junior or third year of high school. U.S. citizenship is required. Scholarships can be used for all fields of study. Actual award amounts vary.

National Young Arts Foundation

Website: https://www.youngarts.org
Additional Information: This talent search competition is open to high school students between the ages of 15 and 18 (or in grades 10 through 12) with talent in the arts such as dance, writing, music, theater, visual arts, and jazz. Awards can be used for any field of study. To apply, you must be a citizen or permanent resident of the United States or its official territories (e.g., Puerto Rico).

Optimist International Oratorical Contest

Website: http://www.optimist.org (Select *Who We Are \ Scholarship Contests*)

Scholarships for Middle Class Students

Additional Information: This scholarship is based on your ability to prepare and present a four to five minute speech on a specific topic within a timed period. Contestants, who must be no more than 19 years of age at the time of contest entry, must speak about the official oratorical contest subject which changes each year. For example, one year's contest subject was, "Why My Voice is Important." Contest is open to citizens of the US, Canada and the Caribbean. You must enter the contest through your local Optimist Club. To get contact information for your local Optimist club, visit the website for additional information. Students must compete in several levels. Visit the website for more details. Award amounts range up to $2,500. *Author's Personal Note:* I competed in the Optimist International Oratorical Contest for several years at various levels beginning in the sixth grade, usually winning at each level but not the final level. Although I did not win the $1,500 award available at that time, I did gain invaluable experience in public speaking and in writing speeches which also helped me to write essays. These are very important skills to have especially if you want to win scholarships. It will help you in both interviews (the ability to speak well in public) and in preparing essays.

1 – Exploring Scholarships in Grades K - 12

Optimist International Essay Contest

Website: http://www.optimist.org (see *Who We Are\Scholarship Contests*)

Additional Information: This is a multi-level essay writing contest. Student winners at the district and international level win scholarships. Contestants must be no more than 19 years of age at the time of contest entry. Contest is open to citizens of the US, Canada and the Caribbean. You must enter the contest through your local Optimist Club. To get contact information for your local Optimist club, visit the website for more details.

OppU Achievers Scholarship

Website: https://www.opploans.com/scholarship
Additional Information: Founded in 2016, this scholarship provides $2,500 for the current or future education costs of high school students and students who are enrolled at least part time in college, graduate, professional, or trade school. Applicants must also have a cumulative GPA of at least 3.0 on a 4.0 scale and submit an essay that tells the organization in 500 words or fewer, why you're an achiever. For example, can you answer yes to any of the following questions: Have you created opportunity for yourself? How have you created opportunity for others? Did you start a small business? Are you the founder of a community program? How did you overcome the odds and

Scholarships for Middle Class Students

make your dreams—or the dreams of others—come true?

Princeton Prize in Race Relations

Website: https://pprize.princeton.edu
Additional Information: The program recognizes and rewards high school students who have had a significant positive effect on race relations in their schools or communities through their volunteer activities. Students can win a $1,000 cash prize. See website for details and to learn about previous recipients.

Profile in Courage Essay Contest

Website: www.jfklibrary.org (see
Learn \ Education \ Profile in Courage Essay Contest)
Additional Information: In recognition of one of President Kennedy's most important legacies, this contest is designed to promote the involvement of young people in the civic life of their country. High school students in the 9th through 12th grades can participate in this essay contest, by writing a compelling 1000 word (maximum) essay and citing at least five sources on the meaning of political courage. Registration forms must be submitted with the essay and are available on the website. The first place winner and the nominating teacher will be invited to receive awards at the Kennedy

Library in Boston. Awards range from $100 to $10,000.

Project Yellow Light Scholarship/Hunter Garner Scholarship

Website: http://projectyellowlight.com
Additional Information: High school and college students who want to encourage fellow students to develop safe driving habits can enter the Project Yellow Light scholarship competition. Your entry, which will consist of a video, billboard design or radio spot designed to motivate, persuade, and encourage your peers not to drive distracted, can win you up to $8,000 for your education. The winning video may be turned into an Ad Council PSA that will be distributed nationally to 1,600 TV stations. The winning billboard design may be displayed on Clear Channel Outdoor digital billboards across the U.S. and the winning radio spot could be shared on iHeartRadio's national network. Visit the website for additional details and requirements.

The Prudential Spirit of Community Awards

Website: http://spirit.prudential.com
Additional Information: This program, sponsored by Prudential in partnership with the National Association of Secondary School Principals (NASSP), recognizes students in grades 5 – 12 who have demonstrated exemplary community service.

Scholarships for Middle Class Students

Local honorees are selected at participating schools and organizations in November, and from these winners, two state honorees are chosen from each state and the District of Columbia. State honorees receive an award of $1,000, an engraved silver medallion, and an all-expenses-paid trip to Washington, D.C. National honorees receive an additional award of $5,000, an engraved gold medallion, a crystal trophy for their school or organization and a $5,000 grant from The Prudential Foundation for a non-profit, charitable organization of their choice. Although this program is not officially a scholarship, the funds you win, if you're an avid volunteer, could add nicely to the money in your college fund to pay for your educational expenses.

Regeneron International Science and Engineering Fair

Website: https://student.societyforscience.org
Additional Information: Students worldwide in grades 9 through 12 or equivalent, compete in an Intel ISEF affiliated science fair to win the right to attend the Intel ISEF and earn up to $75,000 at Intel ISEF each year.

Scholastic Art & Writing Awards

Website: http://www.artandwriting.org

1 – Exploring Scholarships in Grades K - 12

Additional Information: This program is designed to recognize outstanding talent among students in the visual arts and creative writing. Students submit individual works as well as art portfolios and writing portfolios for this competition. Check the website for entry details in the fall. Awards range from $500 to $10,000.

Sodexo Foundation

Stephen J. Brady STOP Hunger Scholarships
Website:://us.stop-hunger.org/home.html or http://www.sodexofoundation.org (see *Grants and Scholarships*)

Additional Information: Stephen J. Brady STOP Hunger Scholarships are open to students in kindergarten through graduate school who are enrolled in an accredited educational institution in the United States. The scholarships are available to students who have performed unpaid volunteer services impacting hunger in a community within the United States at least within the last 12 months. Additional consideration is given to students working to fight childhood hunger. A Community Service Recommendation is required for this application form so ask recommenders (who must not be family members) for their recommendations early.

Scholarships for Middle Class Students

Sons of the American Revolution Joseph S. Rumbaugh Historical Oration Contest

Website: https://www.sar.org (see *Education*)
Additional Information: Oratory competition for high school freshmen, sophomores, juniors, and seniors who submit an original 5 to 6-minute oration on a personality, event, or document of the American Revolutionary War and how it relates to the U.S. today. Oration must be delivered from memory without props or charts. For more information and complete rules, visit the website. Awards range from $200 to $3,000.

"Stuck at Prom" Contest

Website: http://www.stuckatprom.com
Additional Information: Contest is open to U.S. citizens who are high school or home-schooled students at least fourteen years of age who attend a high school prom in the spring wearing complete attire or accessories made from Duck-brand duct tape. Entrants must enter the "Dress" or "Tux" category and submit a color photograph with their entry form and other required documentation. Winners will be selected based on a variety of criteria, including originality, workmanship, use of Duck tape, use of colors, and creative use of accessories. Award amounts range from $100 to $10,000.

1 – Exploring Scholarships in Grades K - 12

TeenDrive365 Video Challenge

Website: http://www.teendrive365inschool.com/teens/video-challenge

Additional Information: In this contest, students who are at least 13 years of age and enrolled in grades 9 through 12 can win up to $15,000 and the chance to work with a film crew to reshoot your winning video entry into a public service announcement (PSA) for TV. Winning entries are based on teen video submissions encouraging others to avoid making bad decisions while driving such as texting.

U.S. Senate Youth Program

The Hearst Foundation
Website: https://ussenateyouth.org

Additional Information: Open to high school juniors or seniors holding a student office. Students must be currently elected to one of the following offices: student body president, vice president, secretary, or treasurer; class president, vice president, secretary, or treasurer; student council representative; or student representative to district, regional, or state-level civic organization. For an application contact your high school principal or state education administrator. Visit the website to find more information about your state's education administrator and the program details. The

Scholarships for Middle Class Students

organization's advice to interested students is to apply in your junior year so that you will have two years of eligibility, rather than one year if you apply as a senior. Award is a $10,000 college scholarship and an all-expense-paid trip to Washington, DC to experience national government in action. Visit the website at the beginning of your junior or senior year for additional details and current deadlines.

Veterans of Foreign Wars of the United States Voice of Democracy Annual Audio Essay Contest

Website: http://www.vfw.org (Select *Community\Youth and Education\Youth Scholarships*)
Additional Information: This scholarship contest is open to grade 9 through 12 students who write and record a three- to five-minute essay addressing the assigned theme, which changes each year. Previous assigned themes have been "I'm Optimistic About Our Nation's Future," "Freedom's Obligation," "Reaching Out to America's Future," and "What Price Freedom?" To participate in this contest, visit the website for more information, speak with your high school counselor, or contact your local VFW post. Scholarship awards range from $1,000 to $30,000. Submissions should go to your local VFW post. Visit the website to find your local post.

2

Exploring Opportunities for Middle Class Students Currently in College

There are also opportunities for middle class students currently enrolled in college to obtain additional funding to continue or complete their education. These include various types of scholarships, grants, prizes and awards. See below to get an idea of the opportunities available and to get started on your college funding journey today!

<u>The Christophers Annual Video Contest for College Students</u>

Website: https://www.christophers.org/video-contest-for-college-students
Additional Information: In this yearly contest, students enrolled in undergraduate or graduate college classes, full or part time, can create a film or video (5 minutes or less in length) to communicate the message and mission of The Christophers and the belief that one person can make a difference. Any genre or shooting style is acceptable and must be submitted for upload onto the contest site or as a link. Prizes range from $100 to $2,000.

Scholarships for Middle Class Students

> ### A FEW IMPORTANT ITEMS TO REMEMBER
> - Do not rely solely on the following scholarship list. It is best to use the strategies described in the chapter, "Searching for Additional Scholarships" to uncover the most opportunities available to you.
> - Some programs change their application requirements and eligibility guidelines. Please review their websites carefully for any changes.
> - Programs can and do stop awarding scholarships or suspend their scholarship programs. Don't get discouraged. You can still find available scholarships. But please know that there are no guarantees about the availability of a given scholarship, or that you will win it.
> - Follow us on Facebook (http://www.facebook.com/scholarshipworkshop) and Twitter (@ScholarshipWork) for frequent alerts on new scholarships and upcoming deadlines. Join our mailing list to get the latest updates about scholarships and other helpful information. Text "SCHOLARSHIPINFO" to 22828 or visit our website to join.

College JumpStart Scholarship

Website: www.jumpstart-scholarship.net
Additional Information: This scholarship is open to 10th through 12th grade high school students, college students and non-traditional students who are U.S. citizens or legal residents. You must be attending or planning to attend an accredited 2-year, 4-year or vocational/trade school in the U.S. and be committed to using education to better your life and that of your family and/or community.

College Is Power Scholarship

Website: http://www.collegeispower.com/scholarship.cfm

Additional Information: This scholarship is available to students 17 years of age or older who plan to start a program of higher education within the next twelve months or who are currently enrolled in a program of higher education. You must be a full- or part-time student, attend a campus-based or online program and be a citizen or permanent resident of the United States. Award amount is $1,000.

Collegiate Inventors Competition

Website: http://www.invent.org (see *Competitions*)
Additional Information: This competition recognizes, encourages, and rewards students to share their inventive ideas with the world. To compete, you must be enrolled (or have been enrolled) full-time in any U.S. or Canadian college or university at least part of the 12-month period prior to the date the entry is submitted. For teams, which can have up to four students, at least one member must meet the full-time eligibility criteria. The other team members must have been enrolled on a part-time basis (at a minimum) sometime during the 12-month period prior to the date the entry is submitted. Your entry must be your original idea and product. See website for complete entry requirements. Awards vary up to $10,000. Although not technically a scholarship, cash prizes can be used however you choose including paying for college.

Scholarships for Middle Class Students

Create-A-Greeting Card Scholarship Contest

Website: www.gallerycollection.com/greetingcardscontests.htm or www.gallerycollection.com/greeting-cards-scholarship.htm

Additional Information: This $10,000 scholarship contest is open to all high school AND college students AND members of the armed forces who are enrolled during the time-period of the contest in an academic program designed to conclude with the awarding of a diploma or a degree. To participate, applicants must create a design for a Christmas card, holiday card, birthday card or all-occasion greeting card. Legal residents of the fifty (50) United States, the District of Columbia, American Samoa, Guam, the Commonwealth of the Northern Mariana Islands, the U.S. Virgin Islands, and Puerto Rico are eligible to enter. International students who have a student visa to attend school in the United States are considered legal residents and are also eligible to enter.

DoSomething.Org Easy Scholarship Campaigns

Website: http://www.dosomething.org (see *Scholarships*)

Additional Information: DoSomething.org is a nonprofit for young people focused on social change for causes such as bullying, homelessness, and cancer. To apply for a scholarship, you need to complete a campaign and prove it with pictures of you in action during the campaign. They have many campaigns featured on the website. The scholarship program is open to U.S. and Canadian citizens 25 and under and does not require a minimum GPA. Winners are chosen through a random drawing.

Dr. Pepper Tuition Giveaway

Website: https://www.drpeppertuition.com
Additional Information: Students between the ages of 18 and 24 can win up to $100,000 in this giveaway by submitting a 1-minute video explaining their goal. Submitted videos are judged as winners based on the following:
- How you want to make an impact with your degree/education
- Inclusion of Dr. Pepper (not mandatory, but recommended)
- Impact the tuition prize could have on your life, your community, or the world
- Overall presentation quality

Frame My Future Scholarship Contest

Website: http://www.diplomaframe.com (search for "Frame My Future Scholarship Contest") or https://www.diplomaframe.com/contests/frame-my-future-scholarship.aspx
Additional Information: This contest is open U.S. citizens enrolled in community college,

Scholarships for Middle Class Students

undergraduate, or graduate school attending a U.S. college or university full-time in the current academic year. To qualify, you must submit an original creation of poetry, photography, ink, collage, painting, mixed media, or graphic design to share what you want to achieve in your personal and professional life after college. Students can win up to $5,000. Finalists are judged based on their entry and description. Winners are ultimately chosen by online vote. For additional information and current deadline, visit the website.

HOTH SEO Scholarship Program

Website: https://www.thehoth.com/seo-scholarship
Additional Information: HOTH is offering current college students and high school seniors accepted to an accredited university an opportunity to win a $1,000 scholarship. To enter, students must write an essay with a minimum of 1000 words on the topic of, "How Companies Can Take Advantage of Digital Marketing." For more details, visit the website.

Law Offices of Randolph Rice Scholarship

Website: https://ricelawmd.com/about/scholarship/
Additional Information: The Law Offices of Randolph Rice Scholarship awards a $1,500 scholarship each year to rising sophomores, juniors, or seniors who are enrolled at a four-year

institution of higher learning, or a high school senior who has committed to attend an accredited U.S. college or university. Applicants must use data from government, private agencies or non-profits, to create an infographic and submit it to enter this scholarship competition. Infographics will be judged based on originality, creativity, and proper use of sources.

"Leading the Future II" Scholarship

Website: http://www.scholarshipworkshop.com
Additional Information: The "Leading the Future" Scholarship is designed to elevate students' consciousness about their future and their role in helping others once they receive a college degree and become established in a community. It is open to high school seniors or current college undergraduates who are U.S. residents. Visit the website to apply online.

OppU Achievers Scholarship

Website: https://www.opploans.com/scholarship
Additional Information: Founded in 2016, this scholarship provides $2,500 for the current or future education costs of high school students and students who are enrolled at least part time in college, graduate, professional, or trade school. Applicants must also have a cumulative GPA of at least 3.0 on a 4.0 scale and submit an essay that tells

Scholarships for Middle Class Students

the organization in 500 words or fewer, why you're an achiever. For example, can you answer yes to any of the following questions: Have you created opportunity for yourself? How have you created opportunity for others? Did you start a small business? Are you the founder of a community program? How did you overcome the odds and make your dreams—or the dreams of others—come true?

Project Yellow Light Scholarship/Hunter Garner Scholarship

Website: http://projectyellowlight.com
Additional Information: High school and college students who want to encourage fellow students to develop safe driving habits can enter the Project Yellow Light scholarship competition. Your entry, which will consist of a video, billboard design or radio spot designed to motivate, persuade, and encourage your peers not to drive distracted, can win you up to $8,000 for your education. The winning video may be turned into an Ad Council PSA that will be distributed nationally to 1,600 TV stations. The winning billboard design may be displayed on Clear Channel Outdoor digital billboards across the U.S. and the winning radio spot could be shared on iHeartRadio's national network. Visit the website for additional details and requirements.

2 – Opportunities for Current College Students

Scholastic Art & Writing Awards

Website: http://www.artandwriting.org
Additional Information: This program is designed to recognize outstanding talent among students in the visual arts and creative writing. Students submit individual works as well as art portfolios and writing portfolios for this competition. Check the website for entry details in the fall. Awards range from $500 to $10,000.

Sodexo Foundation

Stephen J. Brady STOP Hunger Scholarships
Website:://us.stop-hunger.org/home.html or http://www.sodexofoundation.org (see *Grants and Scholarships*)
Additional Information: Stephen J. Brady STOP Hunger Scholarships are open to students in kindergarten through graduate school who are enrolled in an accredited educational institution in the United States. The scholarships are available to students who have performed unpaid volunteer services impacting hunger in a community within the United States at least within the last 12 months. Additional consideration is given to students working to fight childhood hunger. A Community Service Recommendation is required for this application form so ask recommenders (who must not be family members) for their recommendations early.

.

3

Searching for Additional Scholarships

Your search should include the following three areas:
- The library
- The Internet
- Local sources: the local search should involve searching for funds available in your community, state, and region.

For a comprehensive search that gives you the best and most opportunities to win scholarship money, devote close attention to all three!

Library Search

To start your scholarship journey, you should go to the nearest library. Once there, do the following:
- Look for scholarship directories such as the *Ultimate Scholarship Book* or *Scholarships, Grants & Prizes* from Peterson's.
- Search for books such as *Winning Scholarships for College* that go beyond the standard listing found in a scholarship directory. The focus for books of this type is to help you learn how to win scholarships. As a result, they may have limited listings but each listing would include as much additional information on winning the scholarship as possible.
- Search for newspaper articles about scholarships. Newspapers such as *USA Today* periodically have

3 – Searching for Additional Scholarships

articles about getting money for college. To find articles in sources like these as well as the magazines above, use the library's online database or microfiche. In addition, an Internet resource you can use would be Google Alerts.

Internet Search

You can use the Internet in many ways to get college information and find the money to pay your way. The example listing in this resource gives you a general summary for many types of programs. If the web page you would like to view is no longer available, try an advanced search on Google because the location may have changed. Or, the competition may have been suspended or discontinued due to lack of funding or a new direction. Unfortunately this can happen at any time with any program. To help stay informed about new programs, join The Scholarship Workshop on Facebook (www.facebook.com/scholarshipworkshop) or follow us on Twitter @ScholarshipWork for information about new scholarship programs.

Using General Search Engines

Visit search engines such as Yahoo!, Ask, Bing, and Google. Search for terms such as, "college scholarships," "financial aid," and "scholarships." Each of these search engines will give you a list of websites and articles where the term you searched for is included. This will lead you to specific scholarship program websites.

You can also use general search engines to find out if an organization you have heard about in the news or elsewhere has a web address. For example, if a news article lists a program, put the entire name of the program into the search box of an engine with quotation marks around it. By doing this, you may be able to go directly to their website if the search engine finds a link. Or use Google Alerts (www.google.com/alerts) to get e-mail alerts for recent articles written about scholarships, college, and financial aid.

Advanced Internet Search

Have you ever entered a search term in the main search box of a general search engine and received millions of results or advertising pop-ups that really aren't relevant? An advanced search will help you cut through the clutter. You can use the advanced search function in a general search engine such as Google or Yahoo! to find specific information for your scholarship search. An advanced search helps narrow the results you might get from an Internet search.

Perhaps you want to find a scholarship for students in middle school. The example below shows the information you might include for this type of advanced search. Inputting this information into the Google Advanced search uncovered the *Davidson Fellows Scholarship* among others. You could do a similar search for "elementary" or "high school sophomores" as your exact phrases.

3 – Searching for Additional Scholarships

Advanced Search		
Find Results	all of these words	
	the exact phrase	middle school
	any of these words	Scholarship
	none of these words	

Alternatively, you may want to find scholarship essay contests, awards, or prizes that are not based on need. See below for an example of this type of advanced search. Conducting this advanced search can uncover millions of results for essay contests. You could even narrow the results further based on your state or city to find essay based scholarships near you. Also, to eliminate expired competitions, include the current year as well.

Advanced Search		
Find Results	all of these words	scholarship
	the exact phrase	essay
	none of these words	Need
	any of these words	award or prize or contest

Another possible type of advanced search is one based on finding merit or achievement based scholarships. Merit or achievement scholarships often do not have a financial need component. See below for entries to include for this type of search.

Scholarships for Middle Class Students

For exact phrase, input "merit" to search for merit based scholarships. For another search, input "achievement" for the exact phrase to search for achievement based scholarships.

Advanced Search		
Find Results	all of these words	scholarship
	the exact phrase	merit
	none of these words	need
	any of these words	award or prize or contest

Lastly, another type of scholarship you can search for is one based on submitting a video in a competition. These generally do not have a financial need requirement either. What would this type of advanced search include? Take a look below for an example.

Advanced Search		
Find Results	all of these words	scholarship
	the exact phrase	video
	none of these words	need
	any of these words	award or prize or contest

3 – Searching for Additional Scholarships

Local Search

The local search is one most often ignored by the typical student. Usually someone searching for scholarships uses a few scholarship directories and an Internet search service such as www.fastweb.com. For some students in search of college money, an Internet search service is the only resource used. Although search services similar to www.fastweb.com can be wonderful, you should not ignore other sources to find funding. If your scholarship quest includes directories and the Internet only or even just the Internet, you could be overlooking some valuable scholarship opportunities.

The best way to have a complete scholarship search is to search locally in your community, state, and region as well as using directories and the Internet. Most of the scholarships you find in directories and on the Internet are national which means that if you apply, you are among many others who hope to win the scholarship. This makes winning the scholarship harder because it is more competitive. For many local scholarships the number of applications received from students is much smaller which makes them less competitive. This is probably because local scholarships are generally smaller in monetary value and a lot of students feel they aren't worth the time and effort. Fortunately smaller, easier to win scholarships, do add up and should definitely not be ignored. In my scholarship total of more than $400,000, awards as small as $50.00 were included. And my daughter won a small local

Scholarships for Middle Class Students

scholarship when she was eight years old in the area where we live.

For a local scholarship search, you should do the following.

- Search for community foundations. Visit the Northern Virginia Community Foundation (www.cfnova.org) for an example of a community foundation and to see types of scholarships a community foundation might have. Visit the Internet search section of this publication to learn how to conduct an advanced search for scholarship information.
- Research local clubs and organizations. Examples of these would be the Soroptimist Club, the Optimist Club, Exchange Clubs of America, Daughters of the American Revolution, YMCA/YWCA, the Kiwanis Club, the Rotary Club, the Lions Club, or the Knights of Columbus. Also look for sororities and fraternities. Optimist International, an organization that has local clubs throughout the country, has an oratorical and an essay contest for students under age 19 where they can win up to $2500 in scholarships. I competed in the oratorical contest for the local Optimist Club in my area over 25 years ago and won quite a few awards in the process. Although I did not win the scholarship, the experience helped to develop many of the communication and writing skills that I have used successfully throughout my life.
- Contact companies and banks located in your community. Some may have scholarships available to local residents. Call the personnel or human resource department of these companies to

3 – Searching for Additional Scholarships

inquire if they offer scholarships to students in the community.
- Ask your parents to check with their employers. Some employers offer scholarships to children of their employees.
- If your parents belong to a work-related union, contact the union to find out if they offer scholarships to the children of their members. Union Plus is an example of a union that maintains a scholarship program.
- Contact any organization to which you or your parents belong, local or national, to determine whether they have a scholarship program for their members. Your church or faith related organization might be an example.
- Since some credit unions have scholarship opportunities for their members, you should also contact your credit union, if you have one.
-

4

Applications

For colleges and universities, getting an application is relatively easy. For private organizations and companies, getting an application may require a little more work. However, for some large scholarship programs administered or offered by private companies and organizations, downloading applications from websites and applying online is very popular. Many students prefer applying online because it's quicker and easier. Unfortunately it's also very easy to make mistakes and to give answers, especially short essay answers, that don't reflect a lot of thought. It is also important to note that if you apply online you can't include most of the winning elements as discussed in the next chapter.

If you absolutely must use an online application, follow these guidelines:

- Print online applications first without completing them
- Complete them on paper
- Then transfer your answers from paper to your computer in the online application
- Print the completed application
- Proofread
- If you like everything and have no mistakes, press SEND or whatever button you need to press online to send the application. If you

4 – Applications

can, make a PDF copy of the applications you complete. This can make it easier to review your application to get ready for a potential interview.

5

Winning Elements

What are winning elements? Winning elements are items that set you apart from the crowd. Review the following sections for examples of these winning elements.

Essays

Essays are very important to your winning a scholarship. An essay is where you can really shine and tell those who read it how you feel about a particular issue. An essay can help you to elaborate on activities you've outlined in your resumé/activity list. In fact, incorporating your activities, how they have helped to make you into the student or person you are, and how these activities may have helped others, are important features to include in an essay and make its content come alive for the readers, while showing your best qualities.

Young students who need to write essays may need adult guidance. If you're an adult reading this publication for a really young student, interview him or her about their activities and help them formulate sentences to explain and showcase their activities.

Also, for some contests open to elementary and middle school students, the criteria for winning may be based entirely on an essay. These contests may also have a theme for the essay. Students who can interpret the theme well using their written words can excel in these competitions.

Your Work Samples

If you have done anything extraordinary or award-winning or that has received some type of recognition, include a sample as part of your application package. For example, in my scholarship search, I included an award winning layout from the high school literary magazine where I was the editor. I also included poetry that had won awards as well. In one of my applications, I even included a poem I had written titled, "I Am a Child." I liked the poem and thought it represented my writing style and how I felt about life. It also coincided with my essay where I had written about using my journalism skills (gained through my extracurricular activities) to overcome poverty and destruction in America. The poem which had this line, "I am a child yet I have seen cruelty in the face of kindness," fit the theme of my application essay. For the essay, I had to answer the question, "You are at your 30th high school reunion. The president of the United States is part of your class. Yet, you are the guest of honor. Why?"

Make sure you don't go overboard when including samples of your work as part of your application package. One or two items you feel are appropriate are enough. Don't send anything that won't fit in a 9" X 11" envelope. And most importantly, if you are asked NOT to send anything extra, DON'T.

Articles

These articles could be on you or your activities (even if the article doesn't mention your name specifically). If you have been a part of an activity or if you started an activity that has been written about in your local newspaper or college newspaper, include a copy of the article. Once again, don't go overboard. One article, if you're also sending samples of your work is enough. Two articles should be your maximum if you're not including samples of your work.

Résumé/Activity List

Your extracurricular activities, leadership positions, community involvement, and your being a well-rounded student are very important to winning scholarships. To show your involvement in an organized manner with a résumé or an activity list closely resembling a professional résumé helps scholarship programs and educational institutions see your participation and leadership as a whole unit rather than scattered among a few lines on an application.

One of the best ways students can set themselves apart from others is through their extracurricular activities, especially with those that are community service based. Many organizations are very impressed by students who are involved in the community and in their school or educational institution. To show your involvement in an organized and impressive way, you can include a résumé or activity list with your applications. Although most applications will ask you about your activities and include lines for you to list them, your activities look better when presented as a whole and in a résumé-like format. Some students are using the word processing wonders available today to make beautiful résumés complete with pictures and graphic elements that anyone would be proud to show in a job interview. That's the idea. It's great if you have a scholarship judge looking at your résumé/activity list and not only being impressed by what you've done but also how you presented it. Just make sure you don't overdo it with pictures and graphic elements. Content is the most important factor.

For example, you could organize your résumé in the following manner.

<u>Departmental Clubs/Activities</u>
Here list all activities you are involved in within your school

- Student Council – 2019 to present *List activity and years in which you participated*

- National Beta Club – 2019 *List any positions of leadership held and year held as a subheading*

- Future Business Leaders of America – 2018 to present

Scholarships for Middle Class Students

Honorary Clubs
* List all organizations that you have been inducted into because of outstanding performance *

- *National Honors Society – 2020*

Community Clubs/Service Activities
List clubs or activities within the community

- *Role Models and Leaders Program – 2020 to present*
- *Macon City Volunteer Youth Coach – 2019 to present*
- *NAACP – 2018 to present*
- *Susan G. Komen Race for the Cure – 2018 to present*
- *Community Church Youth Group – 2019 to present*

Work/Internship/Research Experience

- *Laura's Babysitting Services – 2018 to present*

Awards/Honors
*List all the awards you have won.

- *Volleyball Team's Most Valuable Newcomer – 2020*
- *Certificate of Participation – Core Advisory Day – 2020*
- *President's Student Service Award – 2022*

*Items in italics and small type are notes to help you create your own résumé.

You can find other types of résumés in *Winning Scholarships for College*. Different formats are acceptable as long as your résumé is easily readable and well-presented.

5 – Winning Elements

Recommendations

Another area where students can stand out from the crowd is through the recommendations of others. In order to get the best recommendations you need to be careful about who you ask, how you ask, and when you ask. Here are a few tools to help you do that.

First, consider the scholarship you are applying for. Even if the program is not requesting a recommendation, include one anyway especially if the recommendation is a good one or it highlights your community involvement. On the other hand, if a program specifies no additional documentation be included with your application, respect their wishes.

Nearly all scholarship programs are impressed by those with community involvement. If the program is requesting a recommendation, try to get at least one from an individual that fits the nature of the scholarship. For example, if it's for a STEM (Science, Technology, Engineering and Math) type of scholarship, get your physics, chemistry or another teacher in a related field to write one.

In general, you should get recommendations from the following if you can:
- a teacher
- a counselor or administrator
- a coordinator for a community based activity
- your minister or another clergyman if you have one
- anyone other than a relative who can discuss your most impressive qualities in a written format.

Scholarships for Middle Class Students

As you think of people to include on your recommendation resource list, make sure to include a sentence about they how they know of you. This will help you to pick and choose individuals to write recommendations as you begin applying for multiple scholarships. Also, when pondering who you should ask, think about whether the person is accustomed to writing recommendations for students or if they might be a good writer. If they have never written a recommendation and/or they aren't a good writer, your recommendation could be a nightmare or a "one liner."

When you ask for a recommendation, do the following:

- Give a written description of the scholarship and/or program
- Include your résumé and any extras you plan to send with your scholarship application
- Include a self-addressed stamped envelope with two stamps (if the recommendation needs to be sent in the U.S. mail)
- Ask at least four weeks before deadline
- Follow-up to see how they are doing or if they need additional information
- Send thank you notes. You may have to ask again.
- *Winning Scholarships for College* (5th edition) includes a sample letter requesting a recommendation as well as an example recommendation chart to help you keep track of recommendations and their due dates.

6

Crafting Your Essay

For most essays, you can use the following five paragraph format particularly if writing is difficult for you. If writing is one of your strengths, there is no need to follow the five paragraph format. Just make sure your essay is interesting and includes details about your extracurricular activities and/or your life.

I. INTRODUCTION - ONE PARAGRAPH

- Use a quotation, poem, thought, amazing fact, idea, question, or simple statement to draw your reader into your topic.
- The main idea does not have to be stated in the first sentence, but it should definitely lead to and be related to your main idea or thesis statement, which should introduce three main points you will develop in the body of your essay.
- Avoid using statements such as, "I am going to talk about . . . " or "This essay is about . . ."

II. BODY - THREE PARAGRAPHS

- Support the main idea with facts, thoughts, ideas, published poetry, quotes, and other intriguing, insightful material that will captivate your audience.

Scholarships for Middle Class Students

- Present clear images.
- If necessary, use a thesaurus to ensure that you are not using the same words repeatedly. Using a word over and over will become monotonous for your audience and distract them from your subject.

III. CONCLUSION - ONE PARAGRAPH

- Restate the main idea in an original way.
- You can again use a poem or quotation to leave an impression. However, avoid using this tactic in all three parts of the essay. It may appear repetitious and unoriginal.
- Refer to the future in terms of your plans pertaining to the subject of your essay. For example, in an essay describing your future career goals, refer to yourself in the career that you have outlined. This reference should project you, and the ideas you presented in the essay, into the future.

* Special Note - Using quotations or poems can show that you are well read. If your essay looks like a dumping ground for quotes and the words of another, using quotations and poems could show something else entirely. Be selective and look for quotes that are enlightening and profound.

As you become more experienced with writing essays you can expand on the format by including more paragraphs or even reducing the number of paragraphs and abandoning the format. If you start with the basic five paragraph format, it is easy to adapt and change to fit the style of your essay, as I did when I wrote an essay for the Coca-Cola

6 – Crafting Your Essay

scholarship which had nine paragraphs. I also changed the format to write an essay for another scholarship program that had only two paragraphs. You can read both essays and an analysis of each in Chapter 11 of *Winning Scholarships for College*.

Early in your scholarship search prepare two basic essays following the format above. The essays can easily be tailored later to fit most scholarship application essay requirements.

Since many essays require descriptions of you and your future career goals, let's follow the format to write an essay about you; featuring your activities. In nearly all of the essays I wrote to win scholarships, I incorporated information about specific activities in which I was involved. Once you finish, this essay and parts of it (recycling) can probably be used for every essay you write regardless of the question.

If you have an essay you need to write for a scholarship immediately, it will help if you do the following activities first.

- Finish your résumé/activity list if you haven't already. This needs to be done before you begin any essay. Using the information from your résumé/activity list, you should include additional details about your activities to support the main points of your essay. Scholarship organizations are very impressed by students who are involved in various endeavors beyond typical classroom work. Showing your passion and commitment to certain activities by including more information about your

involvement will help you stand out from the crowd of other applicants. Refer to the chapter, "Grades Don't Mean Everything," in *Winning Scholarships for College* for more information and also the "Winning Elements" section in this publication.
- Research the organization or company sponsoring the scholarship or award.
- Learn why the scholarship was established and the mission of the organization. If one or more of your activities fit the reasoning behind why the scholarship was established or the organization's mission you may want to highlight this in your essay.
- Understand the question. Think of several ways you might answer and write them down.
- Look at the scholarship application. What do most of the questions focus on: academics, community involvement, etc.? If an organization asks most of its application questions about community involvement, then try to build your essay around activities you do that benefit the community.

Since you are writing a descriptive essay about you or your future career goals, featuring your activities, the next step is to think of three adjectives that describe you. For each adjective, write down an activity that fits with that adjective. For example, the five paragraph essay format would now look like the following:

I. INTRODUCTION - ONE PARAGRAPH

6 – Crafting Your Essay

    A. Adjective/Noun 1
    B. Adjective/Noun 2
    C. Adjective/Noun 3

II. BODY - THREE PARAGRAPHS

  A. Adjective/Noun 1
      1. Activity 1
      2. Activity 2
      3. Activity 3

  B. Adjective/Noun 2
      1. Activity 1
      2. Activity 2
      3. Activity 3

  C. Adjective/Noun 3
      1. Activity 1
      2. Activity 2
      3. Activity 3

Note: You do not need three activities for each. If you have only two, that's okay.

III. CONCLUSION - ONE PARAGRAPH

    A. Summarize your adjectives and how they relate to you and your activities. Refer to the future.

As you write about activities in your essay, don't just list them as you did with your résumé/activity list. If you do, the essay is really saying nothing more than you already did. When

Scholarships for Middle Class Students

you write about your activities, you should be answering these questions as part of your essay:

1. What is the activity?
2. Who does the activity benefit?
3. When do you participate in this activity?
4. Where do you participate in this activity?
5. How does this activity benefit you or others?
6. Why are you involved in the activity?

Based on the outline, adjectives, activities, and answers to the above questions, you could begin your essay like the example below, assuming the adjectives you chose were self-motivated, energetic, and compassionate:

When I think of the words self-motivated, energetic, and compassionate, I think of myself. For the past seven years, starting in elementary, into middle school and now my first two years in high school, I have participated in many activities that reflect these words. More than just words, they really describe who I am and how I feel about life.

For example, in terms of self-motivation, I built a website and Facebook page for students interested in getting tutors at our middle school and continued maintaining it during high school. Building the website and populating it with insightful content was a frustrating and challenging task I set for myself. It took me most of the summer before my freshman year at XYZ High School, but I finished it to the amazement of my parents and friends. The website, once completed, became a much-needed reference for students in our community to find tutors and other information to help them in all types of subjects. The website also helped the

6 – Crafting Your Essay

upper-class students who became tutors make a little money to get a jump-start on college expenses. Most importantly, for those who weren't interested in charging, the site helped those who just wanted to aid their peers and apply principles they learned in class.

As a freshman at XYZ High School, I began to show more of my energetic traits by participating in several athletic activities concurrently which really challenged my self-motivation and determination, but most importantly helped me to relearn the value of teamwork and cooperation for all endeavors. I joined the volleyball team. I became a varsity cheerleader . . .

The next paragraph would focus on compassionate. The last paragraph would be a summary and conclusion. This essay is an example of a rough draft for a descriptive essay using the adjectives self-motivated, energetic, and compassionate. It still needs work but it's meant to give you an idea of how to structure your essay using the adjectives or nouns you selected and the examples of your activities that could fit the adjectives or nouns you selected.
To get additional information about planning your essays, choosing adjectives, writing about your activities, and writing different types of essays, read *The Scholarship & College Essay Planning Kit.*

7

Other Strategies for Middle Class Students

The following information includes a host of strategies you can use to cut your tuition bill as a middle class student.

- Consider certain majors in science, technology, engineering, or mathematics (STEM) related fields. These fields usually have more scholarship money available to them than others.
- If you can do it without completely exhausting yourself, consider completing four years of undergraduate work in three. Or, make sure you finish in four years instead of five or six years.
- Look at institutions that have a matching grant system. In this system if a student who enrolls has an outside scholarship, the institution may match the amount of the outside scholarships up to a certain amount.
- Go to a community college for the first two years. This should cost significantly less than a four-year institution, particularly if you live at home. Using this strategy could potentially get you a degree from an expensive and possibly

prestigious institution at a fraction of the cost. If you decide to do this, make sure the courses you take during your first two years will transfer to the four-year school you want to attend and that they will count toward your bachelor's degree.

- Research and look at schools that value your interests. For example, if you are considering an unusual major in which a college or university may be starting a department, you may be able to get a scholarship or reduced tuition from them as they begin looking for students to enroll in their new program.
- If you're looking at the top-tier schools such as Harvard, Yale, or Princeton, consider putting second-tier schools on your prospective list as well. When it comes to financial aid, you may get more assistance from the second-tier schools who accept you.
- Look at universities and colleges where your grades and SAT scores will place you in the top 10 to 25 percent of prospective students. To find this information, consult a guide such as *Peterson's Four-Year Colleges* to find statistics such as these for the freshman class and student body. If your grades and SAT scores are in the top tier of the students the school tries to attract, you have a good chance of securing more aid from the school.
- Consider participating in the AmeriCorps program or a similar program, which allows

participants to earn education awards or scholarships in return for some type of service or employment during or after college. For more information about service scholarships, review chapter 14 of *Winning Scholarships for College*, "Scholarships & Awards for Community Service, Volunteering and Work."
- Consider the military as an option to reduce your costs. The U.S. armed forces offer several educational programs:
    o You can attend one of the military academies. If you are accepted to a military academy you can essentially go to college for four years tuition-free while earning a commission.
    o You can enroll in the Reserve Officers Training Corps (ROTC) program while in college. ROTC will pay for your tuition, fees, and books and may provide you with a monthly allowance.
    o You can join the armed forces before you go to a college and use the Montgomery GI Bill to help pay for college expenses once you've completed your military service.

In some instances, you can earn college credit for certain military training. This could possibly reduce the number of classes you'll have to take in college.

www.ingramcontent.com/pod-product-compliance
Lightning Source LLC
Chambersburg PA
CBHW052117110526
44592CB00013B/1651